I0896178

BRANCHES

Branches

MARK TRUSCOTT

Book*hug
ABCDEFGHIJKLMNOPQRSTUVWXYZ
2018

The production of this book was made possible through the generous assistance of the Canada Council for the Arts and the Ontario Arts Council. Book*hug also acknowledges the support of the Government of Canada through the Canada Book Fund and the Government of Ontario through the Ontario Book Publishing Tax Credit and the Ontario Book Fund.

Canada Council for the Arts Conseil des Arts du Canada

Funded by the Government of Canada Financé par le gouvernement du Canada Canada

ONTARIO ARTS COUNCIL
CONSEIL DES ARTS DE L'ONTARIO
an Ontario government agency
un organisme du gouvernement de l'Ontario

Book*hug acknowledges the land on which it operates. For thousands of years it has been the traditional land of the Huron-Wendat, the Seneca, and most recently, the Mississaugas of the Credit River. Today, this meeting place is still the home to many Indigenous people from across Turtle Island, and we are grateful to have the opportunity to work on this land.

Library and Archives Canada Cataloguing in Publication

Truscott, Mark, 1970–, author
Branches / Mark Truscott. — First edition.

Poems.
Issued in print and electronic formats.
ISBN 978-1-77166-451-6 (softcover)
ISBN 978-1-77166-452-3 (HTML)
ISBN 978-1-77166-453-0 (PDF)
ISBN 978-1-77166-454-7 (Kindle)

I. Title.

PS8639.R88B73 2018 C811'.6 C2018-904269-9
C2018-904270-2

PRINTED IN CANADA

I have found a way of watching a thing that shows me what I never see when I look at the thing. If I watch a thing from the sides of my eyes, I see in the thing the shape of another thing.

– Gerald Murnane

Contents

1

2

3

4

1

A branch like a line like a branch

Branch like a line like a branch

A line near artless

Then the
hand moves
over in
front the
then-moved
stills and
shades and
pinions
(some ends
are withdrawn)
you can't
see the
forest for
the trees
you can't
see the
trees without
the hand

An *a* nears another.

The moon brushes a branch shines.

The word world a wood door.

Here in the gaps small white glimpses.

The light it catches the wall's edge.

One belies the others. One quickens.

Here and there there are
faint edges to perceive.

(One is a continuity that
nearly reaches its frame.)

One places one thing next to another
and finds them there.

A sky hangs long overhead, and there is
something there where the eye goes.

Here there is reason applied.

Then a hum amidst bleary street lights.

To draw something out
where attention feathers.

One thing before another one
curls its fronds behind.

Leaves there, and
the sun is pale and distant.

This text set isolate
as if in two dimensions.

If these things, the shape
suggesting a line tracing the

mind's current weave
settles here.

A waterglass. A new glint of light
as the morning sun moves on.

It holds itself and there I find it.
It is a hum as it is a line.

Here is a dark body to help me see.
A leaf catches the light. Shines.

2

Serial

Looking is like
brushing against berries,
remembering their form,
grazing the surrounding needles
with just enough pressure
to hint at pain, knowing
the scene extends
beyond whatever frame
vision can muster, that
the berries' distribution's
the result of everything
inhuman there is,
but that it's still artful
and particular.

Conception

A pale blue glow with
another overlaid. One
infinitesimally closer.
To think is to move within
this delay. To see is to
trace the edges while moving.

Looking

When looking is like
the counterpressure
of graphite on
paper, the thing
seen gives instance
to the division of
dark from
light but with
feathering at the edges
where looking traces
the thing's bend
into the world
it is part of already,
leaving looking alone
with lap,
lines,
paper, pencil.

There

How many lines

in this glimpse

of bare tree? The

sun stands on an

angle of near infinite

variability. It

works its way into

sentences. There's

a large door onto a

small room, and I

want to know

about the tree. It's

there, and my

awareness takes

the form of the

thought that, once

drawn, a line can

never really move

in just one direction.

Writing has surfaces.

The tree has surfaces.

I want to read the tree.

But language has no

core. And the branches'

spread spreads

beyond the branches.

Scene

Trees make sense
of the snow, yet
at a certain vicinity
they too become
inarticulate fields.
The trees are limits
to their own
significance. Their
shapes in relation are
momentarily the mind,
but a swell rises with
looking. It's like
a tongueless appetite
almost. As
neighbourhood sparrows
resist enumeration,
the scene offers itself
completely. The wood
absorbs the light.
The air speaks incessantly
with restless hands.

Dust

I know the familiar
indescribability of the
commonest surfaces.
Porous soil and dirt,
dusty light streaming
off painted wood and
plastic. The hand gets
closer than the mind.
The mind gets this, but
still it feels the need to
understand and trace
its understanding.
It wants to be in the world.
It wants to strike some
impossible balance.
Its interval is very thin.

Metaphor

Thought piled
on thought, or
lensed like
raindrops
clinging
to glass. Their
soft drift down
manifests the feeling
that a thought is
subject to force
albeit subtle and
ideal. How can I
insist on sequence
and orientation when
the body glints
in the grey air?
My breath enters
and withdraws without
settling on a single
threshold. But then it
catches ever so
gently on the
muted gleam.

Corner

A
hush
after
softer
sounds
sounds
like a rounded
corner

3

Conjunction

these marks, we
think, might
illuminate

a shape
in the sun's
alien light

(opaque
to the point
of blind touch)

there is
a tree
there

untroubled
where the air
brushes it

standing
as a pronoun
occupies its space

I am
thinking
about it

still
the shape
is legible

as the
body meets
the light

it is in
the wind
blowing

Sketch

Some of it, I
love your windy
voice, the way
leaves come in
at the edges as
you pull the sky
lower. The air is
colourless. It
disregards my
wishes and
establishes
a continuity
as it meets my
eye and goes no
further. True,
you are only
direction forever
overwhelmed by
place. But as your
breath brushes
the surfaces of
the things I see
I can believe
they face me
briefly. We find
names for them
in our language.
The names abide.

Dry grass
overlaps, forms
shadows
as it bends. An
upturned pail
beside it.

Song

The feeling
we could be
doing something
else is always
there, the
edge that
bespeaks the
thing is
here now
too, rolling
away like
a small
moon into
pale flecks
of unattended
detail. The
thing is
there certainly
but there is
complicated.
To consider
thought's
density (and
thereby
increase it),
to feel
intention
curling around

an edge. To
see this opaque
shaping as
song. I am
in the midst
of something
impersonal
yet subject
to near infinite
revision.
There are cusps,
transitions really,
that suggest
beginnings.
There are
smooth
surfaces
it seems
one can
only buy.

Line

The way a branch
divides the sky

there is a line here.

The space around me
is open like a sky.

I think of myself
as having a body.

This is true in my
dreams too.

We say the mind touches
and is touched.

Some textures are almost
impossible to describe.

The line is something
I can believe I've made.

Its substance is slight but actual.

Untitled

These three things
facing sides nearly
square the space
between vibrating with
irresolvable relationship.

(The page is a
plane. The space
before it lies open.)

Points point toward
woody mass. Lines
align with this or that
surface. The sun shines
in the morning light.

(These relations exceed
every thought, and we think
by forming new opacities.)

Points

There's an edge there where
the space before the word appears, where
sense impression gives onto sequence.
There are bodies out there
before my eyes, two small ellipses.
A series of objects is separated by blanks.
The mind then wants to close them, wants
to feel itself embodied and coddled,
implicated yet free.
A field of relations spreads. It
takes its place relative to paper in the world.

Colour

The time it takes the
i to enter *is* is the
time it takes two ideas
to relate is the time
it takes the sun to rise
to where it is this
instant. I write
last night I watched dark clouds
stream cirrus across the moon.
And now the blue of the sky
like dime candy on my tongue.

The Line

I live in the line the

line is alone it is

a thin condensation of its

own timbre. It is a thing in space

or a break with space

and the beginning

of endless association.

I love the line. Its span and

its breadth, its colour,

its texture, and its tension.

And so I live in the world as if

it too has these qualities, and as if it

– and therefore they – can be

described. Here (there) is

a single vector enacted by looking.

Here is an enunciation to direct the attention

and perhaps define. I want

access to opacity and simultaneously

to preserve it. I watch as my hand takes its

place among the things of the world.

4

Corner

There is grit in my teeth
and the sun-scorched street corner
offers too many ways to leave
this moment of attention.
Its heat is visible to the
imagination. Its light and its
high drum are real. Some-
where someone is tasting a
bitterness on the cusp of becoming
matter. The air filters from here
to there, its edge forever deferred.
The street is sound, yet
the air is insensible. I
want the air to stand for space, but
it won't – the light overflows it.
The light gets close to things
in a way I will never know.
It is idiomatic and necessary.

Earth

It's hard to know the way the
earth is hard where
it's been spat up and
packed down by
backhoe wheels and
other unacknowledged machinery.
The earth here isn't waste, but it is
just dirt (mixed with scraps of rock and
plastic), useful in its capacity
to fill space temporarily designated
to be exposed but
tactfully overlooked. It's
past 3:30 on a rare
free afternoon. Instants
unlatch and spread.
They settle and lose
their outlines. What
I see and where I am
overlap almost
completely now, as the
circumscribed ground
precludes horizon.
The sky grows paler
– chalky.

Simultaneity

As a leaf illuminates
leaves I live a half-
lit life, slipping in and
out among declensions.

There are small stones
there. There's a grammar
throughout the air always
desirous, never fitting.
There are grassblades among
the stones.

As a dry branch
falls, the sun seems to
stay where it is. I live
within these relations
spinning out.

A sentence takes its
place among the scatter, prior to metaphor.
Its particular body helps me settle.
Its shapes and associations jar.

Branches, No Birds

Out the window
bodies form rims
at the limits of sight
and rims form lines
in the mind that
feel like touching.

It (the mind?) is like
an edge of light, but
the light never
seems to end, and
this might be what
lends us our human shape.

A curve or reach
against the
smear of the perceived
tells us we are
inhabiting the world
in addition to thinking.

But I see
through my focus
I make things
lonely. An
inverted glow,
a limb divides the
light, both instantaneous
and reflective.

(A voice amplified but muffled
in a car passes by.)

Integers

Predawn birdsong
anticipates the negative
before light allows sensation
to give it shape. The sound
instances itself, hangs
in isolation, and so waking
is like a burrowing into
the narrowest of intervals.
Meanwhile the mind's clearing
is a collapse of proximity,
distance, and signal.
I don't know how I
feel, but I want to say
that something's stirring.
Something that wants
to be the thing that
reaches to the distance's far
side, to touch the sound
before the light breaks.

Feeling

These sounds at night seem
to make room for the mind
to move around them, but they are
not ideas. They are like
wood blocks. The night is also
sometimes wooden, as is
the mind, but now
the air meets the sounds'
edges precisely. To breathe
is to draw this same air over
one's organs, and to think
of these is to remember the diagrams.
We know intuitively that
to touch is to dwell together
in actual simultaneity –
and so each sensation (each
thought) remembers.
One rarely stops searching
for home.

Drawing

A thought then is
what you imagine it
to be. A mirror
cold to the touch
in the winter-thin
air. Watch the world
somehow abiding itself,
yet it looks like
glass. Its surface like
the threshold
breath crosses.
In and out.
Trace your
teeth (you have
spoken). They're
contiguous. You say:
Hunger is a sign
one can't consume.
There's a world out there.
And there's a residue.

Acknowledgements

Thanks to the editors and publishers of the following magazines and websites for publishing poems that appear in *Branches*, sometimes in earlier form: *Arc*, the Cultural Society, *Dusie*, *Event*, *Illiteracy*, *NOÖ Weekly*, and *The Walrus*.

Thanks to the Ontario Arts Council for its support through its Writers' Reserve and Works in Progress programs.

Thanks to Karen Solie for the careful, sensitive, and insightful reading. Thanks also to all at Book*hug: Tree Abraham, Jay and Hazel Millar, Stuart Ross, and Carleton Wilson. Gratitude to Jeff Latosik and Robin Richardson.

And thanks to Lisa, Lucy, and Sam for putting up with me and believing the sacrifices are worthwhile.

About the Author

Mark Truscott is the author of two previous books of poetry: *Said Like Reeds or Things* (2004), which was shortlisted for the ReLit Award for Poetry, and *Nature* (2010). Poems from *Branches* have appeared in *Event*, *The Walrus* and on the Cultural Society website (cultural society.org). Truscott was born in Bloomington, Indiana, and grew up in Burlington, ON. He lives in Toronto.

PHOTO CREDIT: LISA HEGGUM

Colophon

Manufactured as the first edition of *Branches* in the fall of 2018 by Book*hug

Distributed in Canada by the Literary Press Group: lpg.ca

Distributed in the US by Small Press Distribution: spdbooks.org

Shop online at bookthug.ca

BOOK
PRODUCTION
WAR ECONOMY
STANDARD

Edited for the press by Karen Solie
Copy edited by Stuart Ross
Cover design by Tree Abraham
Typeset by Carleton Wilson